Discovering
WALL PAINTINGS

E. Clive Rouse

Shire Publications Ltd

CONTENTS

The cover illustration and plates 2, 4, 5, 6, 8, 9, 13, 14, 18, 20, 21, 23, and 24 are from scale measured watercolour copies by the author. The cover illustration of King David playing the harp is part of the vault decoration at Longthorpe Tower, Cambridgeshire.

Copyright © 1968 and 1980 by E. Clive Rouse. First published in 1968; second edition 1971; third edition 1980. No. 22 in the 'Discovering' Series. ISBN 0 85263 509 5.

Printed in Great Britain by C. I. Thomas & Sons (Haverfordwest) Ltd, Press Buildings, Merlins Bridge, Haverfordwest.

INTRODUCTION

The impression carried away by many people visiting an English church containing wall paintings often tends to be one of disappointment. Sometimes it is one of bafflement or frustration, even anger. For most wall paintings in smaller country churches in England are fragmentary: many are dirty, neglected, obscure and in poor condition, and difficult to decipher and understand. There are of course many shining exceptions where trouble has been taken to clean and preserve paintings. But even so they are not always easy to interpret. Few churches ever bother to have a leaflet explaining their wall paintings.

Up to fifty years ago English medieval art was a subject almost wholly neglected, the view being that we had nothing to compare with wall paintings on the Continent. There has however been a great revival of interest in English medieval art and architecture of recent years. The wonderful work carried out by the late Professor Tristram, inspired by W. R. Lethaby and W. G. Constable, in uncovering, recording, publishing, and bringing to public notice the great value and interest of English medieval wall painting, cannot be over emphasised. But there has been no small popular book on wall paintings to help the interested visitor. And England is still one of the few countries in Europe that has no official body to look after its treasures in this field. It is still left to the individual whim of incumbents or church councils to bother or not, as they choose, about dealing with wall paintings in their churches. There is grudging support for those who *do* care, from Diocesan Advisory Boards: and a parish may be prevented from actually destroying wall paintings— though even this is not unknown. In recent years the Pilgrim Trust and other charitable bodies have made generous grants towards the conservation of wall paintings, under the general control of the Council for Places of Worship. But money has to be raised by the individual churches concerned: and consequently many paintings deteriorate or fail beyond recovery by inertia and neglect. Much of this is due to lack of understanding of the subject by so many people. And so it is hoped that this small book will do something to point out the interest and importance of ancient wall paintings and their contribution to art, history, sociology and teaching apart from their religious aspect.

PAINTINGS WERE UNIVERSAL
IN CHURCHES

It must be realised, then, at the very start that all medieval churches in this country were more or less completely painted. Not all had many figure-subjects but most had some, as will be discussed later.

It may well be asked, if this were really so, why we do not see more of them. The answer is three-fold. First of all, the medieval artist never intended his painting to last for ever. Paintings were constantly being replaced as they became dilapidated or unfashionable; and as the churches themselves were altered or enlarged, so the need for fresh murals grew. In the second place, all wall paintings, screens and painted carved images were obliterated at the Reformation, the walls being covered with limewash, on which texts were subsequently painted, as will be described later. But the third cause of disappearance of wall paintings is by far the most devastating. Whereas the Reformers in the 16th and 17th centuries contented themselves with obscuring the offending imagery with limewash, the Victorians caused wholesale destruction by prejudice and ignorance, and by the wicked and senseless practice of stripping plaster (whether sound or not) from the walls "to show the beautiful stonework"—which of course was never meant to be seen. The rough rubble masonry and even reasonably good dressed stonework, was deemed unworthy: it was the skeleton, the bare bones of the building which was meant to be decently clothed with plaster and adorned with paintings. Literally hundreds of wall paintings were destroyed in the 19th century in this way.

It is often pointed out that the great proportion of paintings occur in the south east of England, in Norfolk, Suffolk, Essex, Kent, Surrey, Sussex, Buckinghamshire, Berkshire, and so on. What is the reason for this: were there not so many paintings in the North? The answer is that in most of the counties listed above there is no easily accessible good building stone, and the walls tend to be of stone rubble, flint or chalk rubble, which you *cannot* strip, and so the paintings have survived. Whereas in the North, the climate is perhaps more inimical to the survival of wall paintings, and there the stone tends to be better and larger, and the temptation to expose it greater. Consequently any paintings on the plaster so removed have gone for ever.

THE PURPOSE OF WALL PAINTINGS

Most people suppose that the object of having wall paintings in a church was purely for decoration, in the same way as you now hang a framed picture on your dining-room wall. This is not so and should be realised at once. Far too many people merely regard a wall painting from the point of view of its artistic merit. Is it a good picture? This was not uppermost in the mind of the medieval painter. He had two objects in view and they were crystal clear. He was there to be devotional: and he was there to teach.

The first object is obvious and needs no elaboration in an age when there was only one religion and everybody knew all about it, instead of the position today when there are endless religions and sects—or none at all.

The second—the teaching aspect of medieval wall paintings —is not sufficiently realised and perhaps needs more explanation. Up to the end of the 15th century there were no printed books. Service books, and such Bibles and religious books as there were, had to be laboriously written out by hand and were expensive, few in number and only possessed by priv: leged persons. In any case, if books of any sort had been generally available, probably eighty per cent or more of the average village congregation could not have read them—they were illiterate—and the books tended to be in languages they did not understand—Latin and French.

So, how was the harassed parish priest (himself often no scholar) to impress the Bible story, the lives of the Saints and the moral teachings of Christianity on his illiterate flock? This was largely done, or assisted, by the paintings on the church walls—the *Biblia Pauperum,* or Poor Man's Bible, as they have been called. They might be likened to the 'Visual Aids' of modern education, or even to the strip cartoon, intended for quick visual assimilation and not for serious digestion. They had to explain themselves by their pictorial content alone. And to achieve this, certain conventions or deliberate exaggerations were introduced. It is important to understand these, or a very wrong impression of English medieval painting in the average village church will be formed. In the great Abbey and Cathedral churches there is more sophistication: the Monks and Canons and the congregation generally were better educated. The artistic standard is higher, and there was not the same need for conventions for teaching, and for moralities. This is well seen in places like Westminster, St. Albans, Norwich, Canterbury, Winchester and Durham.

But the village congregation needed help. So a complete code of signs, attitudes, attributes and gestures was introduced, simply for ease of recognition. Good people had haloes and were beautifully drawn. Bad people—wicked emperors, torturers, executioners—were often made deliberate caricatures with hook noses, hump backs, comic hats or exaggerated clothes. Crowns, gloves, swords were made larger to emphasise rank, position, authority and cruelty.

There was a complete code of signs and gestures. The *Blessing* is well known, and there are two forms of it, the Greek being the earlier where the thumb and third fingers are together, whereas in the later, the third and fourth fingers are folded in, the thumb and first and second fingers being extended and symbolical of the three persons of the Trinity. *Judgment* was indicated by the open palm: *Condemnation* by the single finger pointing. Two fingers denoted *Power*—often the *manus Dei* or Hand of God emerging from a cloud. The curved finger showed *Speech* ; hands up-raised, *Argument* or *Expostulation* ; hands and arms outspread lower down, *Wonder, Adoration* or polite *Listening*. Again in an early form, the arms are crossed in the *Blessing*. The crossing of the legs was important. It was held to be an interruption of the normal flow of life (as seen on early tomb effigies) and became the attribute of wicked Emperors—the only ones who could do it with impunity. Hands placed together, or clasped in a variety of ways denote *Prayer* or *Supplication*.

Apostles, Saints and Martyrs carry objects or emblems, usually associated with their martyrdom or some prominent episode in their lives, purely for recognition purposes and as a reminder of their lives and deaths.

Another convention decreed that the soul should always be represented by a small, naked figure, rank or status being indicated (somewhat incongruously) by the wearing of crowns, mitres, or tonsure. The medieval peasant or itinerant artist could often get his own back on 'the establishment' by representing Kings, Queens, Bishops, Abbots and Priests in the procession of naked souls being dragged off to Hell, in paintings of the Doom.

Costume is, of course, important. People in the paintings were put into contemporary costume—12th, 13th, 14th century or whatever it may be—so as to aid easy recognition of their rank, status or occupation. And this, as in the brasses, is valuable for dating, and as sociological and historical evidence.

Another convention with which the student of medieval wall painting must become familiar is the 'telescoping' or running together of several moments or incidents of a story into one scene. The gestures in a painting of the Temptation and Fall often suggest in one scene the fact of Eve's temptation, her giving the fruit to Adam, and his eating of it. Salome often appears twice in one scene both carrying in the head of the Baptist in a dish and dancing at the feast of Herod and Herodias. In the miracle of Longinus, four separate moments are often shown in one scene—his blindness by showing one eye closed; his piercing of Our Lord's side on the Cross; his miraculous recovery of sight by drops of the sacred blood falling in his eyes (the other eye open, and his hand pointing to it); and finally his kneeling to acknowledge the miracle and his conversion (see Peakirk).

ARTISTIC STATUS

We have lost such an enormous proportion of our wall paintings that it is difficult to form any accurate assessment of the true artistic merit of English wall paintings as a whole. From the best of what has survived it is clear that there must have been very many paintings of the highest quality in each century from the 12th to the 15th. And these can challenge comparison with many on the Continent. There were well recognised artistic centres or 'schools' in England just as much as on the Continent, East Anglia being prominent in the middle ages, as it was for secular painting in the 18th and early 19th century. Not many murals survive in these places or can be associated with them, and our evidence must be largely based on the production of manuscripts in the *Scriptoria* of various great religious houses that can be definitely attributed to individual places. Of these the most important are Westminster, where the Royal or Court School flourished: St. Albans, particularly under Matthew Paris in the 13th century: Norwich: Bury St. Edmunds: Peterborough: Canterbury: and Winchester. In all these places, except Bury and Peterborough, important paintings do survive.

That there were many other competent artists available for work in humbler places (some of them commissioned by a wealthy Lord of the Manor no doubt and borrowed from distinguished establishments) is shown by paintings in such places as Kempley, Clayton, Coombes, South Newington, Little Wenham, West Chiltington, Chalgrove and elsewhere. But for the average village church, the object was different as artistic competence was of secondary importance.

CHARACTERISTICS OF ENGLISH MEDIEVAL MURALS

This brings me to the consideration of the main characteristics of English medieval painting. And it is above all skill, sureness and purity of outline, particularly in the 13th and early 14th century, when English painting was really freed from Norman and other Continental influences and was at its height, that is the salient feature. Abroad, artists were more concerned with elaborate colouring, and solid filling in of draperies and shading, whereas their English counterparts concentrated on the linear essentials—sometimes the minimum of what was needed to convey the meaning of the subject. Indeed poor artistically, even crude, though some of the English village church paintings are, I find their naïve directness, simplicity and utter sincerity often far more moving and more effective than a more self-conscious and elaborately finished work of art.

The Painters

Who were these men? For the most part they remain unknown, at least those responsible for paintings in humble village churches, probably journeymen painters moving from place to place.

The names of a number of artists and craftsmen working under Royal Patronage in the 13th and 14th centuries have survived in the Royal household accounts—the *Liberate* and *Close Rolls*. Under Henry III and Edward III in particular there are extensive lists of names. Even an account of what they were to paint at Westminster, Clarendon, Windsor, Winchester and elsewhere is given, and the nature and cost of their materials—"Vert de greece" (a copper green): "Squirrel's hair for the painters' pencils" and so on. The name of Matthew Paris himself occurs. He was a remarkable man, Sacrist of the great Benedictine Abbey of St. Albans, a working goldsmith, artist, illuminator, historian, chronicler and church reformer who went on a mission to Scandinavia where his influence was such that many Norwegian paintings of 13th century date show strong English characteristics. The names of such men as Walter of Durham and Walter of

Colchester (the latter himself described by Matthew Paris as *pictor incomparabilis*) are found. His brother Simon and his nephew Richard were also painters with him at St. Albans. Some of these men painting at Westminster and St. Albans were monks. But many were not, like Alan, Master Peter, Master Walter and Master Thomas who were all laymen and were employed by Edward I at Westminster.

Far too many works are attributed to "the monks". It is true that any boy or man showing artistic promise would have been trained in the monastic *scriptorium*—there was nowhere else to learn. He would run errands, prepare inks, paints and parchment and act as scribe in preparing service books, Bibles, psalters and so on. He might become a miniaturist or illuminator: he might paint murals or prepare cartoons for stained glass. But he did not necessarily take orders or become a monk. Many did indeed become travelling artists and craftsmen, their later successors no doubt coming under the control of the Plasterers' or Painter-stainers' Guilds in the City of London and other places.

Technique and materials

Mention of some of the painters' materials in the last section raises the question of the technique and materials employed in English medieval wall paintings. Murals are often loosely termed frescoes. Indeed all frescoes are murals, but by no means all murals frescoes. The term fresco ("fresh", or "wet") implies a particular technique hardly ever found in England, but common on the Continent, particularly in Italy, Spain and Greece. The artist and plasterer worked together. The rough outline (called the *sinopia*) was set out in bold strokes on a basic coat of plaster. This was then covered by a thin finishing coat of plaster on which the artist worked, from a cartoon, while it was still wet, the pigments sinking right into the surface. Only so much was put up as the artist could cover while it was in the right condition. That is why many Italian wall paintings can be seen to be in rectangular sections, and the haloes are often in slight relief. Italian frescoes are often executed on a gypsum plaster, whereas in England it is almost always a lime plaster, the finished surface sometimes being polished. The early paintings at Kempley, and the Sussex group of Hardham, Clayton and Coombes are largely in this technique. Some others have become frescoes, *fresco buono*, almost by accident, probably through the dampness in most English church walls! The fresco technique was evidently found unsuitable over here, owing to poverty of walling materials and inimical climatic conditions. A fresco will last almost indefinitely, if it is on the inside of a solid marble wall in a sunny climate. But it is a very different matter on thin chalk rubble in damp and cold conditions.

The method employed in England is the *secco* technique. In other words the whole wall was completely plastered and given a finishing coat or painting surface in lime-putty. This would have been damped and painted on with basic earth colours, with a clear lime water as vehicle, fixed in all probability with skim milk (casein) which was certainly used with limewash. Egg tempera, or occasionally oil, or parchment size was reserved almost exclusively for manuscript painting, and screens or monuments over gesso, though some of these media are not unknown in murals.

The pigments were of the simplest. Oxides of iron are the commonest—red and yellow ochre, which even in themselves had a wide range, the red ochres going almost from purple to pale red. Lime white and lamp or charcoal black gave an added variety. Vermilion, a sulphide of mercury is found, but this was a difficult and expensive colour to make and is unstable in lime painting, tending to blacken in certain conditions. Greens were generally a copper salt. Blue is rare and is usually an azurite, though lapis lazuli is not unknown.

The skilful mixing of only two colours, plus black and white at Coombes shows what a rich range and effect can be produced—deep red, down to the palest pink: deep yellow, almost brown, through to the palest cream: grey, and a colour you would almost swear to be blue, but is in fact black and white with a touch of red.

Occasionally the technique of using a dark under-painting for flesh tints was employed in work of exceptional quality. (St. Albans, Little Wenham, Longthorpe, etc.)

Later paintings tend to have a wider range and more subtle colours: but being often derivative are not always so permanent.

DOMESTIC OR SECULAR PAINTINGS

We have been concerned so far almost entirely with wall paintings in churches. This is not surprising, because hardly any domestic paintings of medieval date survive. But they must have been common in most larger houses. Reference has already been made to painters working at Westminster, Windsor, Clarendon and Winchester, for Royal patrons. These were not merely, or indeed mainly, in the churches, but in the apartments of the Royal castles or palaces.

It is one of the great tragedies of the last century that the old Palace of Westminster was destroyed by fire in 1834. The Painted Chamber, the Antioch Chamber, the Queen's Chamber and other apartments were completely painted, and the paintings renewed at different dates. They are meticulously documented, and some records were made before and after the fire, showing the work to have been of the highest quality. Most of the subjects were biblical. There is no reason to suppose that most castles and great houses of medieval date were not similarly decorated, but most of the castles are now ruinous or destroyed, and the larger houses so altered at later dates that no paintings survive.

At Windsor in 1965 a fragment of painting (part of a series of roundels with Apocalyptic scenes) was found in what had been an ante-room or great chamber connected with Henry III's Great Hall. At Saltford Manor, Avon, a fragment of a wheel (probably of Fortune) and an Annunciation survive. At Cothay in Somerset there are several fragments, including a Tournament scene, and a fox hanged on a gibbet by geese—part of the story of Reynard the Fox popular throughout the middle ages (15th century).

But by far the most remarkable survival is the complete room or Great Chamber of Robert de Thorpe at Longthorpe Tower near Peterborough, giving us an idea of the scope and richness of painting that must have been common even in modest houses, let alone great ones, in the middle ages. The paintings were found just after the end of the 1939-45 war where the Home Guard had loosened some whitewash and distemper. The entire room is covered with paintings of superb quality of about 1330. It has been described as representing 'a spiritual encyclopaedia', combining biblical, moral and didactic and even secular subjects fashionable at that particular date. There is the Nativity: the Apostles' Creed with a commentary: the symbols of the Evangelists with King David playing the harp amid a group of other instruments: the Three Living and Three Dead: the Wheel of the Five Senses: the Wheel of Life or Seven Ages of Man: the Labours of the Months: St. Anthony: St. Paul: and two throned figures and a bestiary subject together with heraldry and birds. It is now in the hands of the Historic Buildings section of the Department of the Environment and can be visited at the usual hours.

The 16th and 17th century saw much painting in smaller houses. And oddly enough when figure subjects were frowned on in churches, they occur quite often in houses—the Prodigal Son: Tobit and the Angel: Elijah fed by Ravens: Moses

11

and the Egyptian: David and Goliath: Judith and Holofernes are all found. The Nine Worthies were a favourite subject (Amersham, and Harvington Hall, Worcs.). But by far the greater number of domestic paintings of late Tudor (Elizabethan) and Jacobean date are decorative, often with a frieze having text panels and various forms of painted representations of panelling. There are many examples in black and white in the classical manner in the style known as 'the antique' or 'grotesque', clearly derived from Italian sources, and many were no doubt copied from title pages of books often via the Low Countries. Such painting may be seen at the Golden Cross, Cornmarket, Oxford. A great scheme like the painted frieze in the Bodleian Library and in Bishop Cousin's Library, Durham, 17th century, where there are portrait medallions of eminent figures in the various fields of academic learning, are unique. These portraits (over 200 at Oxford) were copied from books containing collections of engraved portraits of worthies.

The remarkable building at Piccotts End, Herts., has paintings of about 1500 in one room, and of Elizabethan date in another. In early times this house was thought to be a Pilgrims' Hostel between Ashridge, where there was a famous relic of the Holy Blood, and St. Albans, shrine of the protomartyr.

WHERE TO LOOK FOR PAINTINGS

In general terms, any church which retains its ancient plaster, heavily coated with limewash, may have wall paintings. The top layers will be of post-Reformation texts, concealing earlier, medieval work beneath. A specialist should always be called in before any redecoration or structural work involving disturbance of such wall surfaces is begun. It is perfectly easy to make tests and discover whether there are any remains of ancient painting present.

Only two or three subjects occur with any regularity in the same places. These are the Doom or Last Judgment above the chancel arch (though there are many exceptions to this, of course): St. Christopher is almost always found near or over a doorway or on a length of wall opposite the main entrance. Many churches have more than one St. Christopher, repainted sometimes on opposite walls as the side of entrance was changed, or structural alterations made a change necessary

(Poughill [2], Glapthorne [2], Little Hampden [4]). St. George often accompanies St. Christopher, either adjacent to or opposite him, (Broughton, Padbury).

There was always a Lady Chapel or Lady Altar at the East end of one of the aisles, and paintings connected with the Life of the Virgin may be found here (Chalfont St. Giles and many others). Window splays are a favourite place for painting single figures of Saints or single scenes (Little Kimble, Frindsbury, Kingsdown, Chalgrove, St. John's, Winchester, Hailes, etc.).

If the position and dedication of ancient altars or chantries in a church is known, it can almost certainly be assumed that paintings connected with that will have existed. (For a discussion of the whole question of subject-matter, see below.)

If anyone wishes to see what an untouched church looks like, that is obviously covered with wall paintings of half-a-dozen periods, some appearing through layers of limewash, they should visit Inglesham in North Wiltshire, near Lechlade. This church was a favourite with William Morris, who lived at Kelmscott not far away. It is due to his efforts that no heavy-handed Victorian restoration ever took place there.

Finally, in this introductory section, I would make a plea for patience and understanding of fragmentary paintings, and the preservation of every scrap possible. The student must get his or her eye in. Every piece may provide important evidence and information when we have lost so much. Treat them like the small, individual pieces of a great jig-saw puzzle, in themselves meaningless or difficult to interpret. But you do not throw the pieces away on this account, or the whole picture will never be completed.

THE SUBJECT-MATTER OF MEDIEVAL WALL PAINTINGS

At first sight, it might seem that the range and variety of the subjects and themes met with in English medieval wall painting was almost limitless. But careful analysis suggests that this is not really so, and that the artists were working within a fairly limited, stereotyped framework.

The subject-matter can therefore be roughly grouped under five main headings, which it will be useful to consider in detail. These are: (1) Purely decorative schemes, either on their own, or in association with figure-subjects. (2) The Bible story, Old and New Testament. (3) Single figures of Saints, Apostles, Martyrs, etc. (4) Lives of the Saints in a number of scenes. (5) Moralities, or moral and didactic or allegorical themes usually containing warnings against particular sins or modes of life. In other words, Christianity was brought down to earth, brought up to date, and interpreted in terms of everyday life.

(1) Decorative Schemes

It was not always possible or even desirable to have all the wall surfaces covered with figure-subjects: and so a great deal of purely ornamental painting is found. Rough rubble or stone surfaces, and even good, finely-jointed ashlar, was never left exposed. It was deemed unfinished and unworthy. Plaster was carried right over the window and door reveals, or the stonework was limewashed. The most fearful damage was done, and endless wall paintings were destroyed by the Victorian practice of stripping plaster to reveal rough walling that was never meant to be seen. This point cannot be too much emphasised. Only in 1968 evidence has been found in excavations at York Minster of exterior stone surfaces plastered, and lined out with thick, painted imitation jointing.

The most common painted wall treatment was the masonry pattern, or imitation stone joint. This, with variations such as double or single vertical or horizontal joint-lines, and ornament in the blocks themselves, like roses, scrolls and various flowers and tendrils, is found from the 12th to the 14th century. The earlier work is usually the simpler. It can be found over large parts of the 12th century work at St. Albans Cathedral. Even such an important building as the Chapter House at Christ Church Cathedral, Oxford, only had figures in roundels in the centre of the vault: all the rest was covered by a very simple single-line masonry pattern, with a little scrollwork of 13th century date. The chancel at Haddenham, Buckinghamshire, had a complete masonry pattern scheme. Duntisbourne Rouse in Gloucestershire had a similar scheme. The earlier work at East Wellow, Hampshire, is all masonry pattern, with considerable variety; and in fact some 'stoning and roses' as it is often called, can be found in an enormous number of churches.

The scroll was another important decorative motif; and its evolution and development are valuable in dating. It occurs from the earliest 12th century to the end of the 14th, both on its own as a dado or for outlining windows, doors and arches, as well as for framing or dividing figure subjects. Some of the earliest scrolls are to be found at Clayton and Plumpton,

14

Sussex. Risby in Suffolk has subjects on the North wall divided by a repeated scroll, as well as in window-splays, 13th century. At Stoke Orchard, Gloucestershire, the scrolls are unique, the upper differing from the lower, and each changing its character every few feet. Scrollwork is combined with masonry pattern at Bledlow and Weston Turville, Buckinghamshire, in the nave arcade spandrels.

Arches were often picked out in blocks of alternating different colours—red, yellow, black and white—and were sometimes stippled over in an attempt to represent marble. The chevron was another popular ornamental feature.

Backgrounds were often diapered with small decorative devices, such as roses (cinquefoils, sexfoils, etc.), stars (Stoke Orchard), crosses (Chalfont St. Giles), fleurs de lys, etc. These developed into more elaborate motifs, sometimes clearly painted with a stencil, which became virtually a brocade pattern, and are generally confined to the very late 14th and the whole of the 15th century. They most often accompany St. Christopher and other figure-subjects (Corby, Lincs.).

Heraldry was often used not only for its decorative value, but as a reference or tribute to lords of the manor, local great families or benefactors to the church, and as such is very valuable historically. Elaborate schemes of this sort can be seen at Hailes (Glos.), Chalgrave (Beds.), and Ampney Crucis (Glos.) as well as in many isolated examples.

(2) The Bible Story

This is by far the most extensive and important group of paintings, for obvious reasons. The first essential in the teaching and upholding of Christianity is the basis of its Faith as contained in the Bible, both Old and New Testament.

For some reason in this country the Old Testament is found less than the New: and it is confined to comparatively few scenes. At Hardham, Sussex, there is a fairly extensive series with the Temptation, Fall, Expulsion and various rather unusual versions of the Labours of Adam and Eve. At Chalfont St. Giles (Bucks.) we find part of a Creation scene (animals and birds) and the Fall and Expulsion from Eden, all with diapered backgrounds and scrollwork, first half of the 14th century. At Bledlow (Bucks.) Adam digs and Eve spins with a distaff, also 14th century but later. Cain and Abel appear on window splays at Kingsdown, Kent. We know from the Royal household accounts of the time of Henry III that the History of the Maccabees was among the many

15

subjects represented in the Painted Chamber at the Old
Palace of Westminster (destroyed by fire in 1834). For some
reason the major prophets and some of the great stories of
the Old Testament, like Moses, Noah's Ark, the Tower of
Babel, the Children of Israel and the Red Sea, David and
Goliath, Nebuchadnezzar, Joseph, Daniel in the Lions' Den,
the Burning Fiery Furnace, the Walls of Jericho, Sampson,
and so on, seem to find little place in English wall painting,
though frequent on the Continent. Such things of course are
found in English manuscripts and in carving, particularly
Sampson and the lion.

The New Testament bulks very large, whether there are
single figures of Christ, the Virgin and so on, or individual
scenes like the Nativity, Baptism, Crucifixion, Resurrection,
or Ascension; or series of Cycles of the Nativity, Infancy,
Life of Christ or Passion, the first and last being the most
frequent. The ordinary visitor must not be put off by the
inclusion of some rather strange and unusual scenes in
Nativity series particularly in some of the very early paintings like those at Hardham and Coombes in Sussex, where
the Angel's appearance to Joseph in his dreams is shown.
The Fall of the Idols on the Flight into Egypt, and the
worship of the animals at the Manger, mostly culled from
various versions of the Apocryphal Gospels, also appear.
There are very many fine examples of both individual scenes
and Nativity or Passion Cycles. A few may be instanced: the
series of Crucifixions and scenes concerning the Virgin
(Annunciation, Virgin and Child, Coronation) on the West
faces of the great Norman piers on the North side of the nave
in St. Albans Cathedral; Peakirk, Cambs; Pickering,
Yorks.; West Chiltington, Sussex; Fairstead, Essex; Winchester, Hants. (Holy Sepulchre Chapel). One of the best
series of Passion scenes and the Life of the Virgin is at
Croughton, Northants, 14th century; another is in the
chancel at Chalgrove, Oxon.

Another subject frequently found is the Tree of Jesse or
the ancestry of Christ—a literal tree springing from Jesse's
side, Kings and Prophets in the branches, and the Virgin and
Child at the top.

It is curious that the Miracles and Parables appear very
seldom. The Marriage at Cana (the turning of water into
wine) and the Raising of Lazarus, and Jairus's daughter
(Copford, Essex) are amongst the few miracles represented.
While of the Parables, Dives and Pauper (or Dives and
Lazarus, as at Ulcombe, Kent), is one of the few known to

16

1. Stoke Dry, Leicestershire. St Christopher and the Martyrdom of St Edmund in the south chapel. Fourteenth century.

2. Breage, Cornwall. This warning to sabbath-breakers shows the tools of various trades, if used on Sunday, inflicting injuries on the body of Christ. Late fifteenth century.

3 (right). Durham Cathedral. St Cuthbert in the Galilee Chapel. Twelfth century. (By permission of the Dean and Chapter of Durham.)

4 (above). Canterbury Cathedral, Kent. St Paul at Malta, shaking the viper off his hand, a painting in St Anselm's Chapel. Before 1174.

5 (left). Coombes, West Sussex. A figure supporting a beam and a 'double axe' pattern on the soffit of the chancel arch. Circa 1100.

6. Peakirk, Cambridgeshire. A warning against the sin of idle gossip and scandalmongering — a devil on the shoulders of two gossiping women. Fifteenth century.

7 (above). Little Missenden, Buckinghamshire. St Christopher and the Life of St Catherine on the north wall of the nave. Circa 1300. The scroll border is earlier.

8. Coombes, West Sussex. The lion symbol of St Mark, turning to face a central figure of Christ in majesty. Early twelfth century.

9. *Corby Glen, Lincolnshire. St Anne and the Virgin Mary. Fourteenth century.*

10. *Battle, East Sussex. The scheme on the north wall of the nave, depicting the life of St Margaret of Antioch. Thirteenth to fourteenth centuries.*

11. *Battle, East Sussex. Two of the panels from the St Margaret of Antioch scheme. (Photographs by Ralph Wood.)*

12. Passenham, Northamptonshire. The north-west corner of the chancel showing part of Sir Robert Banastre's great scheme of prophets and evangelists, 1628, with contemporary roof and stalls.

13. Padbury, Buckinghamshire. The miracle of St Edmund's head and the wolf. Fourteenth century.

14. Stoke Orchard, Gloucestershire. Part of a Life of St James the Great and his encounter with Hermogenes the Enchanter, with unique decorative borders. Thirteenth century?

15. Pickering, North Yorkshire. The Life of St Catherine on the south wall of the nave. Late fifteenth century.

16 (below). Fairstead, Essex. The Passion Cycle above the chancel arch, showing the triumphal entry, the last supper, the betrayal and other scenes. Late thirteenth century.

17 (above). Peakirk, Cambridgeshire. The scheme of painting on the north wall of the nave and the north aisle, showing the Passion Cycle and a St Christopher, and in the aisle the Three Living and Three Dead. Fourteenth century.

18. Peakirk, Cambridgeshire. A detail from the Passion Cycle, showing Longinus piercing Our Lord's side and miraculously receiving his sight.

19. *Salisbury, Wiltshire. The repainted Doom in St Thomas's church. Late fifteenth century.*

20. St David's Cathedral, Dyfed. Beneath Bishop Gower's rood screen, an owl and two magpies - idle chatterers mocking wisdom. Circa 1330.

21. Ulcombe, Kent. The parable of Dives and Lazarus. Late thirteenth century.

22 (above). Winchester Cathedral, Hampshire. A detail from the vault of the Guardian Angel's Chapel. Mid thirteenth century.

23 (right). Longthorpe Tower, Cambridge-shire. King Reason, a detail from the Wheel of the Five Senses. Circa 1330.

24. *Llantwit Major, South Glamorgan. St Christopher and the Holy Child. Late fourteenth century.*

me. The Good Samaritan and the Prodigal Son occur oddly enough in post-Reformation domestic paintings.

(3) Single Figures of Saints

Single figures of Apostles, Saints and Martyrs are of very frequent occurrence; and to this group can be added representations of single scenes in their lives (St. Christopher carrying the Christ Child across the stream; St. George killing the dragon; St. Catherine and the spiked wheel; St. Margaret emerging from the dragon.)

It should be clearly understood that these figures were not selected on any basis of decorative or pictorial value, or because of some current fashion. In pre-Reformation England the attributes of particular saints were well-known, and they were invoked for particular things and on particular occasions. St George, the patron saint of England, was a type of manly Christian virtue and chivalry, and when you saw his picture on the church wall you were reminded of these qualities, and said your intercession for your husband who was on the Crusades, or your son or your brother who was fighting in the French wars.

St. Christopher, the patron saint of travellers, was invoked for those setting out on pilgrimage, or on a journey, which in medieval England could be difficult and even dangerous. But he was more than this: his story teaches salvation through service; the windmills, the churches, houses, fishermen and boats introduced into the scene served as reminders that his legend was applicable in the everyday world. This can be well seen at Baunton, Glos., and Shorwell in the Isle of Wight. The introduction of a mermaid into the picture often puzzles people. The mermaid comes straight from the Bestiaries—those collections of beasts, real and imaginary, having a religious or moral significance of which there are many examples in manuscripts. The mermaid was an evil creature, a siren to lure men to destruction, and her presence in St. Christopher paintings is intended to suggest temptation and distraction of the Saint from his task. (The Pelican feeding her young from her own breast and the Phoenix rising from the flames, also found in the Bestiaries, are both Christian symbols, of the Crucifixion and Eucharist and the Resurrection, and may be seen at Belchamp Walter, Essex.)

St. Catherine was an immensely popular figure, and as patron saint of clerks and of learning was much venerated in an age when knowledge was power and in the hands of comparatively few.

St. Margaret was invoked by women in childbirth. St. Nicholas was the patron saint of children (Santa Claus) and of sailors. St. Anthony was venerated especially by basket-makers, and his aid was sought in cases of 'St. Anthony's Fire' (erysipelas). At Longthorpe Tower near Peterborough he is shown in the wilderness amongst birds, trees and rabbits during his vision of angels alternately working (making baskets) and praying, and who say to him 'do this and you shall have everlasting life'.

The presence of other single figures of Saints is probably to be accounted for by individual choice or because the person responsible for commissioning the painting had a particular devotion to a particular saint. Thus we find a wide variety—St. Martin dividing his cloak with the beggar (Nassington, Northants.; Chalgrave, Beds.); St. Clare, St. Francis, St. Bernard (Little Kimble, Bucks.), St. Eligius or St. Eloy (the patron saint of smiths, blacksmiths in particular). To these must of course be added single figures of the Apostles and Evangelists, often in association with the dedication of a church. The range is thus very wide, and the matter of identification by their symbols or actions a continual interest.

(4) Lives of the Saints

This class of painting follows on naturally from the last, but instead of a single figure or a single scene from a saint's life (like St. Martin dividing his cloak with the beggar; St. George slaying the dragon; St. Nicholas rescuing the three boys from the pickle tub; St. Anne teaching the Virgin to read, and so on) we have a series of scenes forming a longer or shorter version of that saint's 'History'. This obviously gave greater scope to the artist, to the parish priest to expound a good story, and to the congregation for interest as well as devotion.

The scenes were sometimes in two or more tiers, and were treated in a manner not unlike the modern strip cartoon—if one may use such an analogy. Some very early examples (the Sussex group of Clayton, Plumpton, Hardham and Coombes) have the scenes divided by fantastic architectural motifs. Others run on without vertical divisions, being bordered at top and bottom in the manner of the Bayeux tapestry, or the tiers divided by dado bands or scrolls, (Risby, Suffolk). These are sometimes very difficult to sort out, especially when the paintings are fragmentary as they so often are. Often the clue is to be found in the fact that the figure at the end of one scene and the beginning of the next have their backs to each other, the interest or action of each scene being in the centre, with the main participants facing each other (as at Stoke Orchard, Glos.).

In other cases the scenes are contained within arches (West Chiltington), or are divided by simple vertical lines or frames as at Sporle (Norfolk), Little Missenden (Bucks.), Tarrant Crawford (Dorset).

Much of course depended on the space (or the money) available in deciding the number of scenes, incidents or miracles to be shown. Some, like the Life of St. Catherine at Sporle, Norfolk, were extensive, in this case some twenty-seven scenes are included. Others were a mere epitome of the main events, like the 'Life' of St. John Baptist at Chalfont St. Giles, where only three scenes appear, and two of those are telescoped into one.

Probably the most extensive series, and certainly the best artistically and one of the few that are documented, is the Life and Miracles of the Virgin, the scenes divided by figures of female saints in elaborately painted representations of canopied niches, on the walls of Eton College Chapel. The College accounts show that they were painted by one Gilbert and by William Baker and his assistant(s) between 1478 and 1482. Their life was a short one; for in 1560 the College barber was paid 6s. 8d. (half a mark) to obliterate them with whitewash. Thus they remained for nearly three hundred years, until the Prince Consort, visiting the Chapel, one day, found workmen busily engaged in scraping them off the walls. He was able to halt the work, but not before almost the whole of the upper row of scenes on each side had been destroyed. They were then concealed behind the sham Gothic stall canopies put up by George Street, until they were revealed once more by Professor Tristram under the inspiration of Provost Montague James, probably the greatest medieval scholar of his generation. A similar series is in the Lady Chapel at Winchester Cathedral.

The cult of the Virgin was enormous in the middle ages, and representations of her life and miracles must have occurred in most churches, especially in connexion with the Lady altar. These range from the humblest work like those at Chalfont St. Giles and Bradwell Abbey, through the fine series at Croughton, to the supreme examples just mentioned above, and including the exquisite Virgin and Child in the Chapel of the Bishop's Palace at Chichester. It is almost solely in scenes like this, and the Weighing of Souls, that any tenderness or humanity is allowed to creep in.

Next in popularity are probably St. Catherine and St. Margaret (a wonderful series has been cleaned and revealed at Battle, Sussex), and St. Thomas of Canterbury (Thomas à Becket) who became almost a national saint, as did St. Edmund. Then there are those 'local' saints whose legends are less familiar and consequently more difficult to identify, like St. Swithin of Winchester, whose restoration, intact, of a basket of eggs, broken by hooligans, to a poor woman, is shown at Corhampton.

Sources

It will obviously be asked, what were the literary sources for the different versions of the lives and miracles of the Saints. But in this small book there is clearly no time to enter into an academic discussion of medieval literature or manuscript sources. That is one of the many facets of this whole subject that the student must follow up for himself. There were many such sources available to the priest and artist, like the *Libelli* or small lives of various saints and martyrs, or Vincent de Beauvais' *Speculum Historiale* and others. But probably the most familiar and most used was the compilation known as the Golden Legend or Lives of the Saints—the *Legenda Aurea*—of Jacobus de Voragine, Archbishop of Genoa, about the middle of the 13th century. He in turn drew on earlier sources such as St. Jerome, Eusebius and others, and the work in manuscript form soon spread all over Europe. It contains accounts of lives or references to some 160 or 170 Saints, Apostles, Martyrs or Festivals of the Church. Today we are familiar with it in the superb English of Caxton's translation of 1483. It is interesting that even at that date, doubts were beginning to creep in as to the literal authenticity of some of the fantastic happenings recorded. For instance, in the Life of St. Margaret of Antioch, she asks that, while in prison, the devil that is tempting her to take the easy way out, forsake her Christianity and yield to the wicked Provost's demands, should be shown to her in bodily form. Caxton continues, "And then appeared a horrible dragon and assailed her . . . and it is said that he swallowed her into his belly, she making the sign of the Cross. And the belly brake asunder, and so she issued out all whole and sound." And then the charming aside, "This swallowing and breaking of the belly of the dragon is said that it is apocryphal". The scene perhaps accounts for St. Margaret being invoked by women in childbirth; and it is one most frequently represented (Tarrant Crawford, Dorset; Piccotts End, Herts; Battle, Sussex.)

Other and much older and more obscure sources were used for the remarkable Life of St. James of Compostella (James the Great, the Apostle) at Stoke Orchard, Glos., for the paintings were executed before the Golden Legend was compiled or at least became current. There are some twenty-eight scenes surviving, and there were originally many more. Some do not occur in the Golden Legend at all and others appear out of order. Sources thought to have been used are the pseudo-Abdias and the compilation of Pope Callixtus II.

In all the foregoing subjects, the Nativity and Passion Cycles in particular, a very close link is observable between them, with their episodic treatment, and the medieval religious drama, performed at Festivals on moving waggon stages or Pageants. Scripts of some of the York, Coventry, and Wakefield Cycles might well have inspired the mode of presentation of many scenes, like the Nativity set shown by life-size single figures at Corby (Lincs.). There King Herod, cross-legged on his throne, might have stepped straight out of the Coventry Shearmen and Tailors' Play.

"Where can you have a more greater succor
Than to behold my person that is so gay,
My falchion, and my fashion with my gorgeous array."
Dr. Hildburgh has also noted close affinities with the ala-basters and the Passion and Nativity plays.

(5) Moralities

The last group into which I have divided the subject-matter to be found painted on English church walls is the Morality or Warning. This group is in many ways the most interesting of all, providing as it does a much more human element and a closer insight into the medieval mind, its processes of thought and its teaching methods. The moralities are more-over more closely based on contemporary literature and teaching.

The Doom. I have placed in this class the great paintings of the Doom or Last Judgment without which no church was complete, and which were usually situated (though space sometimes dictated otherwise) in the most prominent position fully facing the congregation over the chancel arch. The sub-ject is of course a Biblical one, but in the paintings it becomes a great allegory, literally represented, and that is why I have included it here. Although details vary, the general composition is constant. It is treated as a great drama in a number of scenes.

Christ is in the centre, judging the quick and the dead. He is seated on a rainbow whose ends emerge from conventional clouds. He is robed to display the five wounds, and He blesses with one hand and holds up the open palm in judgment. His feet are on a sphere, divided so as to denote dominion over the elements of earth, air and water. Scrolls often bear the words, to those on His right hand (the North or left side from the spectator's point of view), "Come ye blessed of my Father, and inherit your kingdom . . ." To those on the other side are addressed the ominous words "Go ye evil-doers into eternal fire". Angels usually bear symbols of the Passion. Groups of the Heavenly Host often flank the central figure and are led by the Virgin and John the Baptist, with the Apostles and Evangelists, while other Angels blow a literal Last Trump.

Lower down is the General Resurrection, with souls (always by convention represented as small, naked figures) rising from graves or coffins, and awaiting judgment. On the North side (supposing the painting to be on the East wall) is represented the Heavenly Jerusalem—a collection of battlemented, gated and towered buildings with St. Peter and Angels receiving the Blessed at the gate. On the South side are the torments of the damned in Hell, where the artist really let himself go, with souls dragged off by a chain, a great gaping mouth, cauldrons, flames, demons, bellows, pitchforks and horrors unimaginable. Often the Seven Deadly Sins are shown in Hell, or on their way to it. What the effect of this was on simple minds may well be guessed. Something of this is expressed in one of Francois Villon's *Ballades,* at his mother's request to invoke Our Lady (late 15th century):

> A pitiful poor woman, shrunk and old
> I am, and nothing learn'd in letter lore.
> Within my parish-cloister I behold
> A painted heaven where lutes and harps adore
> And eke an Hell whose damned souls seethe full sore:
> One bringeth fear, the other joy to me.

Fear and joy: good and evil: life and death—this is really the whole burden of medieval religious painting. Examples of Doom paintings are too numerous to mention: but the great composition over the chancel arch at St. Thomas's Church, Salisbury, though largely repainted in the 19th century, gives a very good idea of the overwhelming awesomeness of the whole subject.

Everyone who has ever noticed a wall painting at all is probably familiar with the strange subject filling the whole West wall at Chaldon church, Surrey. This is sometimes erroneously called a Doom, but should more properly be called the 'Ladder of Salvation', or a kind of schematic representation of the Redemption. Its date is the end of the 12th century, though touched up, and the origins of its theme must date from Byzantine sources. Included in the composition are the Harrowing of Hell or Descent into Limbo or Purgatory; Our Lord taking Adam and Eve by the hand; the Tree of Knowledge; the Torments of Hell; the Seven Deadly Sins, and the Weighing of Souls.

The Weighing of Souls. The Weighing of Souls was sometimes included as part of the Doom, but also quite frequently treated separately. It is all picture language for the idea that at the Last Day one's good deeds will be weighed in the balance against one's bad deeds—a belief not peculiar to the Christian religion, but found also in Egypt and in Classical mythology. This is shown literally with St. Michael holding an enormous pair of scales. The Devil tries to weigh one side down, urging your sins; while on the other the Virgin intercedes by touching the beam or placing the beads of her rosary in the other pan and so weighing it down in favour of the soul, her compassion being underlined by the action. In some cases (Corby, Lincs., Broughton and Little Hampden, Bucks.) she is also shown as sheltering or protecting souls under the folds of her cloak, an idea of French Cistercian origin in the 13th century where she is called *La Vièrge au Manteau Protecteur* or *La Vièrge de Miséricorde*. It is of interest that only in such scenes connected with the Virgin is any tenderness or humanity allowed to creep in. The rest is stern, crude stuff. The times were crude, and if you wished to impress crude and simple people, crude methods had to be employed to bring home the enormity of sin, and its penalties, the rewards of the just, and the uncertainty of life.

Good and Evil. The eternal struggle between good and evil is indeed the paramount theme of most medieval painting, and especially in this group of the Moralities. The Seven Deadly Sins and the Seven Corporal Works of Mercy gave the parish priest the opportunity to expand on this subject. Pride, Envy, Anger, Lust, Covetousness, Sloth and Gluttony on the one hand are balanced by Receiving Strangers, Clothing the Naked, Feeding the Hungry, Giving Drink to the

Thirsty, Visiting the Sick, Visiting Prisoners and Burying the Dead, as in the text in St. Matthew, Chapter 25. At Linkinhorne in Cornwall, the works of Mercy surround a figure of Christ Himself.

The methods of representation are very varied. In early examples (12th century) the struggle is shown as a combat between Virtues and Vices (the Psychomachia or battle of the soul). These are usually armed figures, sometimes on horseback, as at Copford (Essex), Claverley (Salop.) and Pyrford (Surrey). Later, various diagram forms were used. Diagrams were beloved of the intelligentsia in the middle ages as may be seen in many encyclopaedic manuscripts like Queen Mary's Psalter, and the Arundel Psalter. The Tree was a favourite motif, since it has a cycle of growth, leaf, blossom, waning and apparent death or inertia, only to start again in the Spring. Chaucer used the simile for the Seven Sins in his Parson's Tale—the evil stock or trunk that has its roots in the sizzling cauldron of hell: the limbs, branches, twigs and buds representing other sins all stemming from the central stock of Pride. This treatment is shown at Ruislip, London. The Wheel, another diagrammatic representation of continuous or recurrent movement, was another very popular form. There are Wheels of the Seven Sins, of the Virtues (Arundel), of Life, (Kempley and Longthorpe), of Fortune (Rochester), of the Five Senses (Longthorpe) and so on. At Padbury, Bucks. the Wheel treatment is used for the Seven Sins. Pride and her six daughters or the Purging of Pride, where the central figure is speared by Death, is another version (Raunds, Northants., Little Horwood, Bucks., etc.). The Sins and the Works of Mercy are shown in dragons' mouths and in roundels respectively on the West wall at Trotton, Sussex, and there are many examples up and down the country.

Warnings: The Three Living and the Three Dead. Many other moralities take the form of awful warnings against particular sins or bad habits. Of these, one of the most frequently met with is the warning of the transitory nature of earthly rank and riches, known as the Three Living and Three Dead, or, since it seems to originate in a French late 13th century manuscript, *Les Trois Rois Vifs et les Trois Rois Morts*. There is an almost contemporary English manuscript, the Psalter of Robert de Lisle sometimes known as the Arundel Psalter in the British Museum, now thought to date in part from the end of the 13th century, which shows this subject and on which very many wall paintings must have been based. Three Kings, sumptuously robed, one with hawk on wrist, encounter three grisly skeletons, and the following conversation takes place. The Kings: First: "I am afeared". Second: "Lo! what I see." Third: "Me thinketh it be devils three". The skeletons: First: "I was well fair." Second: "Such shalt thou be." Third: "For God's love be warned by me." In other words, no matter how rich and important you may be, death will come, and perhaps sooner than you think. On the Continent, the Kings are usually mounted, out hunting; but in this country more often on foot. The subject is of very wide distribution and frequent occurrence — popular is perhaps hardly the word since various creepy-crawlies, toads, worms, moths and every symbol of decay and corruption are often introduced. It is found from Wensley in Yorkshire to Charlwood in Surrey; from Tarrant Crawford in Dorset, and Widford in Oxfordshire to Raunds (Northants.), Longthorpe and Peakirk (Cambs.) and Pickworth (Lincs.), with numerous fragmentary examples scattered all over the country especially in Norfolk and Suffolk. Later examples, following the fearful mortality of the Black Death (1348/9), seem to be the more numerous. It is an obvious counterpart to the Dance of Death or Danse Macabre so often found on the Continent.

Warning to Swearers. A subject occasionally found is that of a warning against the sin of blasphemy, or swearing by parts of Our Lord's body, apparently very prevalent in the 14th and 15th centuries. At Broughton, Bucks. and at Corby, Lincs. the Virgin is seated in the centre, holding the dismembered body of Christ, surrounded by fashionably dressed youths either holding parts of the body—bones, feet, heart— or with scrolls containing their oaths. In a window (now gone) at Heydon, Norfolk, they were swearing, "By God's bones that was good ale": "By Gods' heart I will go to town": "By the feet of Christ I will beat you at the dice", and so on. This is referred to by Chaucer in the Pardoner's Tale:

> ". . . The cursed swearers:
> 'Tis grisly for to heare them sweare,
> Our blissed Lorde's bodie they to-teare:
> Them thoughte Jewes rent him not ynough."

At Corby there is the added feature that each of seven youths is accompanied by a devil tempting him to the sin, and there are allusions to the wounds of Christ and the Seven Deadly sins—the whole subject a mass of symbolism. There is an obvious counterpart in the painting of the Seven Corporal

41

Works of Mercy at Ruabon, Wales, where each good deed is inspired by an Angel.

Warning to Sabbath-Breakers. Of much wider distribution is a strange representation of Christ, naked but for a loin cloth, displaying the five wounds, and often covered with drops of blood, surrounded by tools, implements and objects of every sort of trade and occupation .There was a group of five or six in Cornwall, but only Breage, Poundstock and St. Just in Penwith survive. It is found at West Chiltington (Sussex), Ampney St. Mary (Glos.), Hessett (Suffolk), Nether Wallop (Hants.) and many other places. It has been the subject of much learned speculation and discussion in the past. It has been called the Christ of the Trades ; the Consecration of Labour ; Professor Tristram identified it as Christ as Piers Plowman (in allusion to passages in John Langland's work), and there have been other interpretations. A painting in the Church of St. Miniato outside Florence, showing this precise subject of Christ surrounded by tools touching Him, has an inscription beneath it which puts the matter beyond doubt. In translation it reads "Whoso does not keep holy the Sabbath Day and have devotion to Christ, God will consign him to everlasting damnation." The teaching is clear, that by using the tools of your trade and ignoring Christ on His Sabbath Day, you not only inflict injury on the Body of Christ, but condemn yourself to perdition.

Warning against Idle Gossip. A feature complained about (and preached against, as shown by Professor Owst in his *Preaching in Medieval England* and *Literature and Pulpit in Medieval England*) was the evil habit of people chattering and gossiping inside and about the church. Idle gossip and scandalmongering can have far-reaching disastrous effects ; and this is shown by two paintings at Peakirk (Cambs.) and Little Melton (Norfolk) where two women are hard at it, but on their shoulders stands a devil cramming their heads together, and encouraging the evil practice.

There are a number of paintings which do not seem to fit into any particular category, but which clearly have an allegorical or moral significance, and so may be considered here. At Swanbourne in Buckinghamshire is a curious painting showing the states of the Soul before and after death—Angels and devils contending for the Soul and so on, with long inscriptions. The lesson is clear, that if you have lived a thoroughly virtuous life, your place in heaven is assured: if you have been only moderately good there will be a struggle between the forces of good and evil for possession of your soul: but if you have led a thoroughly bad existence on earth, then you are without hope destined for the nether regions. So far the literary source for this interesting painting has not been traced. But the origin of many others is to be found in such works as The Desert of Religion, The Hortus Deliciarum (or Garden of Delights), John Myrc's instructions to parish priests, the poems of Langland, Chaucer and Lydgate.

Many strange birds, animals and creatures are often found on church walls, as at Hailes, Glos., mostly inspired by the Bestiaries as I have already indicated—the Phoenix, the Pelican, the Mermaid. The owl mobbed by magpies has a deeper than purely decorative significance, and suggests the idle busybodies and chatterers of this world mocking at wisdom.

The signs of the Zodiac sometimes appear: and the cycle of Man's earthly activities, the Labours of the Months, as found in such manuscripts as the Calendar section of Queen Mary's Psalter and the Luttrell Psalter.

Some of the well-loved legends, almost like the Fables of Aesop, are strangely absent in wall painting though often met with in wood carving. There was a scene from Reynard the Fox (now destroyed) associated with a St. Christopher at Ludgvan, Cornwall; and a fragment of a fox hanged by geese remains on a wall of the Great Hall at Cothay Manor, Somerset.

Many churches retain a few painted consecration crosses. There were originally twelve inside the building and twelve outside, those inside being painted, and those outside carved or scribed. These were anointed with holy oil by the Bishop in the ceremony of consecration. Radnage, Penn, Padworth, Southease, Iffley, Ulcombe, Fairstead, and many other places retain examples.

POST REFORMATION PAINTINGS

It must not be supposed that painting in churches ceased at the Reformation. It took a different form. The religious upheavals of the reigns of Henry VIII and Edward VI, and of Elizabeth I resulted in a violent reaction against all 'popery', and imagery was frowned on. There was an Order in Council of 1547 for the 'obliteration and destruction of popish and superstitious books and images, so that the memory of them shall not remain in their churches and houses.' All the beautiful paintings were covered by lime-wash, and their place taken by texts of scripture, 'the sentences' as they were called (Creed, Lord's Prayer and Ten Commandments), and the Royal Arms, ordered to be displayed in every church—and still supposed to be—by Henry VIII after the Act of Supremacy. These texts in elaborate frames were constantly renewed, and they and the intervening coats of limewash often enough conceal medieval work.

Since imagery was frowned on, very few figure subjects are found. There are Moses and Aaron, usually associated with the Ten Commandments: the symbols of the twelve tribes of Israel (Stoke Dry, Leics.; Burton Latimer, Northants.; West Walton, Norfolk; Eyam, Derbyshire): and a curious group, Time and Death—an interesting survival of the medieval preoccupation with mortality.

Then there are exceptional examples like Passenham, Northants., where the whole chancel, rebuilt by Sir Robert Banastre in 1626/8, has a contemporary scheme of great magnificence. The major Prophets, Isaiah, Jeremiah, Ezekiel and Daniel representing the foretelling of Christ are on the North; the Evangelists (St. Mark destroyed by the founder's own monument) showing the fulfilment of Christ, on the South; and Joseph of Arimathea and Nicodemus representing the Passion, on the East wall. Bratton Clovelly, Devon, seems to have had a similar but much cruder scheme.

The painting of texts continued right up to Victorian times when they became terribly debased and mechanical, and often painted on tin scrolls tacked up. However, there are many really good Victorian schemes of painting, both pictorial and decorative, and these should always be kept whenever possible.

A remarkable series of 17th and 18th century texts is at Abbey Dore, Hereford, some signed and dated by the painter; and another at Hawkshead, Cumbria, where the actual contracts and the names of the artists survive, dating from the late 17th and early 18th century.

BOOKS ON WALL PAINTINGS

There are not many books generally available on English wall paintings. The older ones are out of print, and some of the more recent are bulky and expensive. The best source for accounts of individual paintings or sets of paintings will be found in the Journals of the various County Archaeological Societies—Berkshire, Oxfordshire, Essex, Suffolk and Buckinghamshire are particularly good in this respect. It is a disgrace that no up-to-date general list of existing or formerly existing wall paintings has been published since Keyser in 1883, a valuable starting-point but now hopelessly out of date. Funds have been made available and the Courtauld Institute of Art are supervising a scheme for bringing Keyser up to date and extending the scope of the survey.

List of Buildings having Mural Decorations. C. E. Keyser, H.M.S.O. 1883.

Mural Paintings in English Churches during the Middle Ages. Frank Kendon. Bodley Head. 1923.

Catalogue of an Exhibition of British Primitive Paintings. Introduction by W. G. Constable. O.U.P. 1924.

English Medieval Painting. Borenius and Tristram. Pegasus Press, 1927.

Medieval Wall Paintings. J. Charles Wall. Talbot Press (n.d.).

English Medieval Wall Painting: the 12th Century. E. W. Tristram, O.U.P. 1944.

English Medieval Wall Painting: the 13th Century. E. W. Tristram. 2 Vols. O.U.P. 1950.

English Wall Painting of the 14th Century. E. W. Tristram, edited by Eileen Tristram. Posthumously published. Routledge & Kegan Paul. 1955.

English Medieval Mural Paintings. A. Caiger-Smith. Clarendon Press, Oxford. 1963.

The Church of St. John the Evangelist, Corby, and its Mural Paintings. E. Clive Rouse. Privately printed by Strangeways Press for Sir Walter Benton Jones. 1941. And in Archaeological Journal, 1944.

The Wall Paintings at Longthorpe Tower. E. Clive Rouse and Audrey Baker. Archaeologia. Vol. XCVI. 1955.

St. Christopher in English Medieval Wall Painting. H. C. Whaite. Ernest Benn. 1929.

The Ancient Mural Paintings in the Churches of Gloucestershire. W. Hobart Bird. John Bellows (n.d.).

Lewes Priory and the early Group of Wall Paintings in Sussex. Audrey Baker. Walpole Society. Vol. 31.

Twelfth Century Paintings at Hardham and Clayton. Clive Bell. Millers Press. 1947.

Wall Paintings in Stoke Orchard Church, Glos. E. Clive Rouse and Audrey Baker. Archaeological Journal Vol. CXXIII. 1967.

Wall Paintings in the Church of St. Pega, Peakirk, Northants. E. Clive Rouse. Archaeological Journal. Vol. CX. 1954.

A SELECTIVE LIST OF CHURCHES ETC. HAVING WALL PAINTINGS

(Where there are extensive examples, or paintings of high artistic importance, the name is marked with an asterisk*.)

AVON
Saltford Manor, Wellow.
BEDFORDSHIRE
Chalgrave*, Houghton Conquest, Marston Moretaine, Shelton, Toddington*, Turvey*, Wymington*.
BERKSHIRE
Aldermaston*, Ashampstead*, East Shefford, Enborne, Eton (College)*, Ruscombe, Stanford Dingley*, Tidmarsh, Windsor.
BUCKINGHAMSHIRE
Bledlow, Broughton*, Chalfont St. Giles*, Lathbury, Little Hampden*, Little Horwood, Little Kimble*, Little Missenden*, Penn, Radnage, Swanbourne, Weston Turville, Whitchurch.
CAMBRIDGESHIRE
Bartlow, Barton*, Broughton, Castor, Chesterton, Chippenham, Ely (Cathedral), Glatton, Hauxton, Ickleton*, Impington, Kingston*, Longthorpe Tower*, Molesworth, Old Weston, Peakirk*, Willingham*, Yaxley.
CHESHIRE
Chester (St Mary on the Hill), Marton, Mobberley.
CORNWALL
Breage*, Poughill, Poundstock*, St Just in Penwith, St Keverne, Sennen.
CUMBRIA
Hawkshead.
DERBYSHIRE
Dale, Eyam, Haddon Hall*, Melbourne, Taddington, Wingerworth.
DEVON
Axmouth, Bratton Clovelly, Exeter (Cathedral)*, Sidbury*, Weare Giffard.
DORSET
Cerne Abbas, Cranborne, Gussage St Andrew, Tarrant Crawford*, Whitcombe*, Wimborne (St Giles Hospital).
DURHAM
Durham (Cathedral*), Pittington.
EAST SUSSEX
Arlington, Battle, Brightling, Patcham, Plumpton, Preston, Rotherfield*, Southease.
ESSEX
Belchamp Walter*, Bradwell (near Coggeshall), Copford*, Fairstead*, Great Canfield, Lambourne, Layer Marney*, Little Baddow, Little Easton, Waltham Abbey, Wendens Ambo.
GLOUCESTERSHIRE
Ampney Crucis*, Ampney St Mary*, Baunton, Berkeley, Cirencester*, Duntisbourne Rouse, Gloucester (St Mary de Crypt), Hailes*, Kempley*, Oddington*, Shorncote, Stoke Orchard*, Stowell, Tewkesbury.

GREATER LONDON
East Bedfont*, Hayes, Ruislip*, Tower of London (Byward Tower)*, Westminster Abbey*, Westminster Palace (St Stephen's Chapel, now in British Museum).

HAMPSHIRE
Alton, Bramley*, Breamore, Corhampton*, East Wellow*, Farnborough, Hartley Wintney (redundant), Idsworth*, Nether Wallop, Portsmouth (Cathedral), Silchester, Soberton, Tufton, Winchester (Cathedral), Winchester (St John's)*.

HEREFORD AND WORCESTER
Abbey Dore*, Dowles Manor, Harvington Hall*, Hereford (All Saints), Hereford (Black Lion Inn), Martley, Michaelchurch Escley, Pinvin, Wickhamford, Worcester (The Commandery).

HERTFORDSHIRE
Abbots Langley, Cottered, Flamstead*, Newnham, Piccotts End (Hemel Hempstead)*, Ridge, St Albans (Cathedral)*, Sarratt.

HUMBERSIDE
Goxhill, Sledmere.

ISLE OF WIGHT
Bonchurch (Old Church), Godshill, Shorwell.

KENT
Bapchild, Barfreston, Bishopsbourne, Borden, Brook*, Canterbury (Cathedral)*, Canterbury (St Mary, Northgate), Canterbury (St Thomas's Hospital)*, Capel*, Cliffe, Dartford, Doddington, Eastry, Faversham, Frindsbury, Halling*, Kingsdown, Lenham, Lower Halstow, Newington*, Rochester (Cathedral), Selling, Stone, Ulcombe*.

LEICESTERSHIRE
Braunston, Cold Overton, Great Bowden, Great Casterton, Empingham*, Lutterworth, Lyddington, Stoke Dry*.

LINCOLNSHIRE
Caythorpe, Corby (near Grantham)*, Friskney, Haceby (redundant), Lincoln (Cathedral), Nettleham, Pickworth*, Ropsley, Stow, Swaton, Swinstead.

NORFOLK
Attleborough*, Burnham Overy, Catfield, Cawston, Crostwick, Fritton (near Long Stratton), Fritton (near Yarmouth), Great Hockham*, Haddiscoe, Hemblington*, Horsham St Faith (Priory), Little Melton, Little Witchingham, Moulton St Mary, Norwich (Cathedral)*, Paston, Potter Heigham*, Seething*, South Burlingham, Sporle, Weston Longville, West Somerton*, West Walton, Wilby.

NORTHAMPTONSHIRE
Ashby St Ledgers*, Burton Latimer*, Croughton*, Doddington, Easton Neston, Easton-on-the-Hill, Glapthorn, Great Harrowden*, Holcot, Nassington, Passenham*, Polebrook, Raunds*, Slapton*, Stanion, Thorpe Mandeville.

NORTH YORKSHIRE
Bedale, Easby*, Pickering*, Wensley.

NOTTINGHAMSHIRE
Blyth.

OXFORDSHIRE
Beckley, Besselsleigh, Black Bourton*, Bloxham, Broughton*, Cassington, Chalgrove*, Charlton-on-Otmoor, Checkendon, Combe, Cropredy, Eynsham, Hook Norton, Horley, Hornton*, Kelmscot*, Kidlington,

Kingston Lisle, North Leigh, Northmoor, North Stoke, Oxford (Bodleian Library), Oxford (Cathedral and Chapter House), Oxford (Golden Cross, and 3 Cornmarket St), Shorthampton, South Leigh*, South Newington*, Swalcliffe, Thame, Widford*, Wood Eaton, Yarnton.

SALOP
Alveley, Claverley*, Edstaston*.

SOMERSET
Cleeve Abbey, Cothay Manor, Farleigh Castle (Hungerford Chapel), Marston Magna, South Cadbury, Sutton Bingham*, Wedmore, Winsham.

SUFFOLK
Alpheton, Bacton, Bardwell*, Boxford, Bradfield Combust, Brent Eleigh*, Chelsworth, Earl Stonham, Grundisburgh, Hessett*, Hoxne*, Lakenheath*, Little Wenham*, Long Melford*, Mutford, North Cove, Risby*, Stanningfield, Stoke-by-Clare, Stowlangtoft, Troston, Wenhaston, Wissington*.

SURREY
Albury, Caterham, Chaldon*, Charlwood*, Pyrford, Stoke d'Abernon, Warlingham, Witley.

WARWICKSHIRE
Stratford-on-Avon (Guild Chapel)*, Stratford-on-Avon (White Swan Inn), Wootton Wawen.

WEST MIDLANDS
Wyken.

WEST SUSSEX
Amberley, Arundel, Boxgrove, Chichester (Bishop's Chapel)*, Clayton*, Coombes*, Hardham*, Trotton*, West Chiltington*, Wisborough Green.

WILTSHIRE
Great Chalfield (Church and Manor), Lacock Abbey, Lydiard Tregoze*, Oaksey, Salisbury (Cathedral), Salisbury (St Thomas's).

It should be understood that there are very many churches where fragmentary or obscure paintings are to be seen. And these the visitor will enjoy discovering and trying to interpret for himself. The list given here is only a summary of the more extensive, interesting or good quality paintings. Where houses are mentioned, it does not mean that they are all necessarily open to the public.

There are of course a number of paintings in Wales (Llantwit Major, Rugg, St. Davids, Ruabon, Colwinston, Llangyby), with many churches having texts; and a very few in Scotland and the Channel Islands, but these are not considered in detail in the present instance.